My birthday

My signature

T0321490

My
AWESOME
Year
Being

9

Published by Collins
An imprint of HarperCollins Publishers
Westerhill Road
Bishopbriggs
Glasgow G64 2QT
www.harpercollins.co.uk

HarperCollins Publishers
1st Floor, Watermarque Building, Ringsend Road, Dublin 4, Ireland

First edition 2020

10 9 8 7 6 5 4 3

© HarperCollins Publishers 2020

ISBN 978-0-00-837263-7

A catalogue record for this book is available from the British Library

ACKNOWLEDGEMENTS
Publisher: Michelle I'Anson
Concept creator: Fiona McGlade
Author and Illustrator: Kia Marie Hunt
Project Manager: Robin Scrimgeour
Designer: Kevin Robbins
Photos © Shutterstock

Special thanks to the children at Golcar Junior Infant and Nursery School

Printed by GPS Group, Slovenia

My AWESOME Year Being 9

Written and illustrated by
Kia Marie Hunt

CONTENTS

HELLO!

Your year being 9 is going to be **AWESOME** now that you have this book to record it in!

You're about to discover **SO MANY** fun activities, projects, recipes, and other exciting new things to try...

Start by writing your name, birthday, and signature just inside the front cover — and draw something awesome!

Near the end of the book, there are blank pages where you can continue with any of the activities, try something again, or just do whatever you like!

Just inside the back cover, track your mood by colouring in a box for each day of your awesome year being 9!

P.S. You might need a grown-up's help to do some of the things in this book, so ask them to read the note on page 128.

~~RULES~~

1. Fill in the pages **in any order** you like.

2. You could use **pencils, pens, crayons** or **paints** to answer the questions. You could also stick in photos or make a collage of different materials. Feel free to make a **mess!**

3. See any uncoloured drawings? Why not **colour them in?**

4. See any white spaces? Why not add your own **doodles?**

5. Complete the book how you want. There's no right or wrong way to express yourself!

6. **HAVE FUN** and remember that you are **awesome!**

ME AND MY AWESOME LIFE

Describe how you **LOOK**.

Are you tall or small? What is the colour of your eyes, hair and skin?

_____

_____

Where do you **LIVE**?

_____

Draw your home, or stick in a photo.

Who do you LIVE WITH?

_____

_____

Draw them here, or stick in photos.

Who got THIS BOOK for you?

_____

(Remember to thank this person... if they got you this book, they're obviously pretty great!)

8 THINGS I LIKED
ABOUT BEING 8

Think about the 8 things you liked the most about being 8 years old, and put them inside the doodles.

You can write or draw.

10 THINGS I'D LIKE TO DO BEFORE I'M 10

Can you think of 10 things you'd like
to do before you are 10? It could be
anything from visiting a place you've
never been to before, to trying a new
food, or maybe even performing in public.
Write them down, then tick the box once
you've done each of them.

You don't
have to do
all this in one
go. You can add
some things then
come back to
it later.

1 .... ☐

2 .... ☐

3 .... ☐

4 .... ☐

5 .... ☐

6 .... ☐

7 .... ☐

8 .... ☐

9 .... ☐

10 .... ☐

SELFIE ART

Let's make some selfie art! Stick in
photos to complete these challenges.

You
can draw
instead
if you
prefer!

A NORMAL SELFIE

This is what
I **look like**.

A SILLY SELFIE

This is me doing
something **funny**!

AN 'USSIE'

These are **group** shots of me with my family or friends.

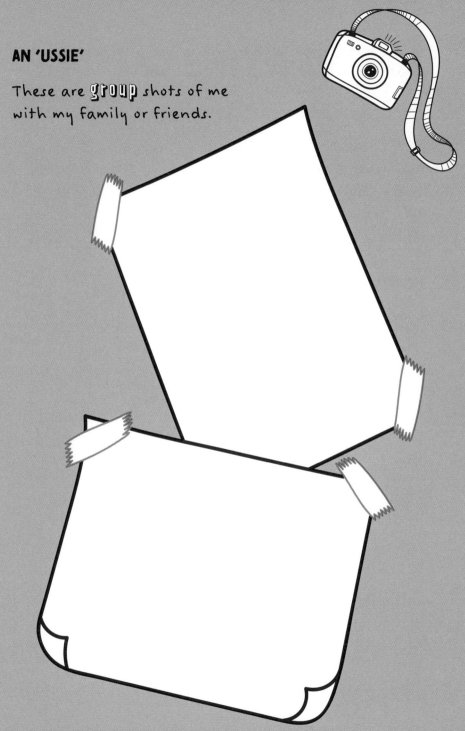

MAKING A TIME CAPSULE

A **TIME CAPSULE** is a small container that you fill with things from your life as it is right now. Once you make a time capsule, you **HIDE IT** away until one day in the future when it will be **OPENED AGAIN**. It's like a present from the past to the future!

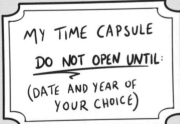

What you will need

- A small container with a lid (e.g. a shoebox).
- Some things from your life now like photos of you and people in your life, photos of the rooms around your home, or a letter to your future self.
  (You could even make copies of the 'Me and my awesome life' pages in this book and add those into your time capsule too!)
- A safe hiding place where the capsule won't be found for a long time (such as an attic, a basement, or the back of a cupboard or wardrobe that no one ever uses!).

Once you have made your time capsule, all you need to do is decide on a **DATE** when it is allowed to be opened again. It could be 1 year from now, 5 years from now, or even 10 years from now!

Seal the lid of the container, then write your name, today's date, and this message on the lid:

MY TIME CAPSULE
DO NOT OPEN UNTIL:
(DATE AND YEAR OF YOUR CHOICE)

WHAT THINGS did you put inside your time capsule?

Write, draw, or stick in a photo.

WHERE did you hide it?

WHAT DATE in the future will you reopen it?

How do you think your **FUTURE SELF** will react to finding the time capsule again after so much time has passed?

MY MUSIC

What kind of **music** do you like to listen to?

. . . .

. . . .

Who are your **top 3** favourite singers or bands?

(If you don't have favourites, just pick some that you like to listen to at the moment.)

1 . . . .

2 . . . .

3 . . . .

What is your favourite **song**?

(This could be your favourite song ever, or just a song that you really like at the moment.)

. . . .

. . . .

. . . .

MY PLAYLIST

Make a playlist of all the **best songs** from your year as a 9-year-old. Every time you hear a song you **really like**, write it down here. Some songs might be ones that have made you laugh, some might remind you of a place or a person, and some might just be songs you think are great!

Name of song	Who sings it

WHAT I'M GRATEFUL FOR...

What are you grateful for? Write down things that make you feel happy and thankful here in your **GRATITUDE JOURNAL**.

You don't have to fill in all the spaces at once, you can come back at any time throughout the year and keep on adding more things that make you feel grateful.

(**Tip:** some things that you're grateful for might be big important things, like your family or your home. But sometimes, you might feel grateful for the little things too, like the weather one day, some food you ate, or just something nice that a person did for you.)

RECIPE: **BONKERS BRITTLE**

It's amazing how much sugar can change when we heat it up and cool it back down again. This bonkers brittle recipe isn't just a recipe, it's a **SCIENCE EXPERIMENT** too!

Ingredients

- 170g of sugar
- 220g of butter
- 1 tablespoon of glucose or corn syrup

- 120g of nuts (almonds or peanuts work very well, but you can choose your favourite!)

How to make

BE SAFE! It is **very** important to get a grown-up to help with this recipe because it includes heating sugar to a high temperature.

1. Line a baking tray with baking paper.
2. Put the sugar, butter and corn syrup into a deep pan on a medium heat.
3. Keep stirring and stirring until it begins to boil, then turn the heat down to low and be very careful in case it splatters.
4. Add the nuts of your choice into the pan and stir.
5. Pour the mixture onto the baking tray.
6. Once it has cooled completely (after about 2 hours), break your brittle into pieces and **enjoy!**

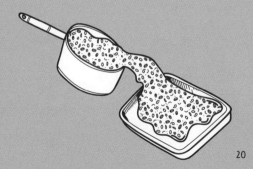

Rate this recipe out of 10

1=Yuck!
10=Yum!

WHO did you make this recipe with?

WHICH NUTS did you use in your bonkers brittle?

How did the mixture **CHANGE** when it was heated and cooled?

What was your **FAVOURITE PART** of this recipe/experiment?

SEASONAL STROLLS

SPRING STROLL

Date: _____

Where did you go for your spring walk?

_____

What signs of spring could you see, smell, feel or hear?

_____

Draw something **spring-like** that you saw on your walk, or stick a photo here:

Return to these pages throughout the year – they're all about going for a walk during different seasons!

SUMMER STROLL

Date: _____

Where did you go for your summer walk?

_____

What signs of summer could you see, smell, feel or hear?

_____

Draw something **summery** that you saw on your walk, or stick a photo here:

AUTUMN STROLL

Date: _____

Where did you go for your autumn walk?

_____

What signs of autumn could you see, smell, feel or hear?

_____

Draw something **autumnal** that you saw on your walk, or stick a photo here:

WINTER STROLL

Date: _____

Where did you go for your winter walk?

_____

What signs of winter could you see, smell, feel or hear?

_____

Draw something **wintry** that you saw on your walk, or stick a photo here:

MY SCHOOL

What is your school called?

_____

What year are you in? _____

How many children are in your class? _____

Describe how you feel about school in 3 words:

Do you have a school uniform?

Describe it, draw it, or stick in a photo.

What 4 things do you like about going to school?

(These could be favourite subjects or classroom activities, things you like to do at lunchtime or playtime, teachers or friends that you like, or anything else!)

1 ....

2 ....

3 ....

4 ....

What 4 things would you like to change about going to school?

(These could be subjects you would like to change or cancel, activities you would like to do differently, school rules you would like to add or remove – you could change anything!)

1 ....

2 ....

3 ....

4 ....

MY FRIENDS

Who are your FRIENDS?

List their names and write down where you met them, and what you like most about them.

Name of friend	Where I met them	What I like most about them

Draw some of your friends as **SUPERHEROES** and label what their **SUPERPOWERS** would be!

BEING AN OUTDOOR CHEF

Maybe you cook for your family all the time, or maybe you've never stepped foot in the kitchen. Either way, this is your chance to be **head chef** for the day, but **with a twist** – you're going to cook **outside**!

Cooking outdoors is such a fun experience, whether you are camping somewhere or just spending an evening in a garden. Use these pages to plan out your menu.

You might want to ask a grown-up to help you find a recipe that you can cook together outdoors. Here are a **few ideas** to get you started:

- BBQ burgers or hotdogs
- Macaroni cheese (on a campfire cooker)
- Baked potatoes
- BBQ skewers with grilled peppers
- Strawberry and marshmallow s'mores
- Corn on the cob

What are you going to cook outside?

. . . .

On the opposite page, list the ingredients you need and how you will make the meal.

BE SAFE! Always ask a grown-up for help cooking outdoors.

Ingredients I need

....

....

....

....

....

How I will make it

....

....

....

....

....

....

Date: ....

Where did you cook outside?

Write, draw, or stick in a photo.

Who did you cook with?

....

Did your recipe go to plan?

....

How did it taste?

What did your food **look** like?

Draw it or stick in a photo.

What was your **favourite** thing about cooking outside?

· ·

· ·

Would you be an outdoor chef again? Why or why not?

· ·

· ·

MY FAVOURITE BOOK

Write down the **TITLE** and **AUTHOR** of your favourite book.

WHAT HAPPENS in the book?

WHY is this book your favourite?

How does reading this book make you **FEEL**?

BEING A 9-YEAR-OLD BOOKWORM

Whenever you read a book, record the title and author here, rate it out of 10, and fill in a **book review**.

Title

Author

Rating

What did you think of the book?

1=Awful
10=Awesome

You can do more book reviews over the page, and on the blank pages at the end of this book!

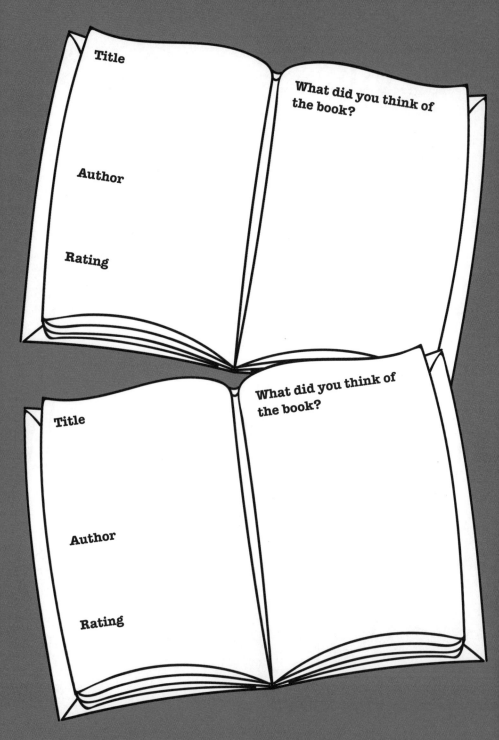

Title

What did you think of the book?

Author

Rating

Title

What did you think of the book?

Author

Rating

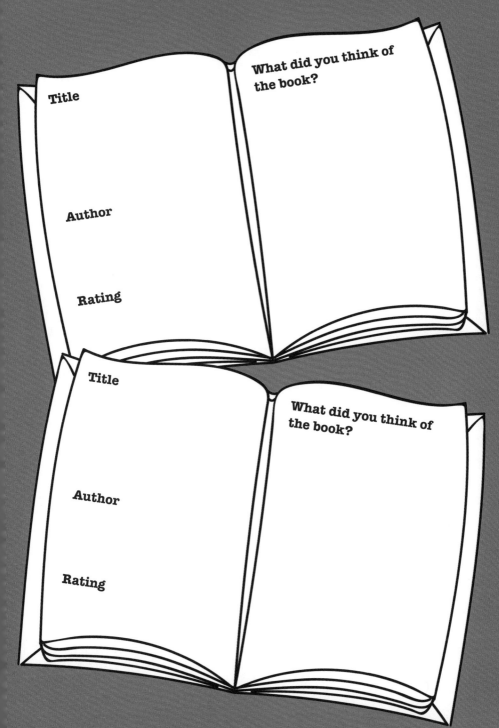

Title

What did you think of
the book?

Author

Rating

Title

What did you think of
the book?

Author

Rating

MY TRAVELS AROUND THE WORLD

What country do you **LIVE** in?

- -

What is your country **FAMOUS FOR**?

(This could be a landmark, a typical meal, a person, a sports team, or something else!)

Write about or draw.

On the opposite page, choose **2** more countries and write about or draw something they are famous for.

(These could be countries you have been to before, or countries you would like to visit.)

Name of country

_____

☐ I've visited before
☐ I would like to visit

Name of country

_____

☐ I've visited before
☐ I would like to visit

MY GREAT ADVENTURE

If you had to **escape** from the country you live in now and go on a **great adventure** to start a **new life** somewhere else, which other **country** would you choose to **live** in?

....

Why would you like to live there?

....

....

....

....

....

....

....

Imagine you have made your great escape and you are now living in your country of choice. What would your **new life** in that country be like?

Think about what things would be **similar** to where you live now and what things would be **different**.

(What food would you eat? What would the weather be like? Would you have to learn another language? How would your culture change?)

Write, draw, or stick in photos.

MY HOBBIES & CLUBS

1. **NAME** of hobby or club:

HOW OFTEN do you do this hobby or take part in this club?

What do you **LIKE MOST** about it?

Draw a picture (or stick in a photo) of this hobby or club.

Fill in these pages with information about 4 of your favourite hobbies or clubs. If you don't have 4, why not try a new hobby or join a new club, then come back and fill in a page later? You don't need to fill them all in at once.

2. NAME of hobby or club:

HOW OFTEN do you do this hobby or take part in this club?

What do you LIKE MOST about it?

Draw a picture (or stick in a photo) of this hobby or club.

3. NAME of hobby or club:

HOW OFTEN do you do this hobby or take part in this club?

What do you **LIKE MOST** about it?

Draw a picture (or stick in a photo) of this hobby or club.

4. **NAME** of hobby or club:

HOW OFTEN do you do this hobby or take part in this club?

What do you **LIKE MOST** about it?

Draw a picture (or stick in a photo) of this hobby or club.

KEEP ON MOVING!

You can stay **active** by playing sports, walking, running, jumping, skipping, dancing... the list goes on!

How often do you **exercise**?

What **kind of exercises** do you like to do?

What is your **favourite** way to stay active?

What is your **least favourite** exercise?

How does exercising make you **feel**?

Try out these exercises and write down how many you can do (or how long you can do them for!).

I can do [ ] press-ups.

I can do the plank for [ ] seconds.

I can do [ ] lunges.

I can do jumping jacks for [ ] seconds.

I can do [ ] squats.

I can skip for [ ] minutes.

These are your 'personal bests' for each exercise.

(You can come back and try to beat them again later.)

GROWING MY OWN VEGGIES

Starting your own **VEGETABLE PATCH** is easy and fun. Plus, veggies always taste so much nicer when you've grown them yourself!

How to do it

1. Ask a grown-up to help you prepare a patch of land in a garden or allotment with some good soil for growing things.
2. Plant some seeds or bulbs for the vegetables you want to grow. Here are some great ideas for fast-growing, tasty veggies:

   - Beans
   - Carrots
   - Courgettes
   - Peas
   - Radishes
   - Tomatoes

3. Keep coming back to check on your vegetable patch often, as you will need to water it regularly (especially if there hasn't been much rain).
4. As your vegetables begin to grow, take photos of their progress.
5. When you have fully-grown vegetables, try them. You'll probably notice that they have a lot more flavour than vegetables from a shop! Why not use them in a recipe?

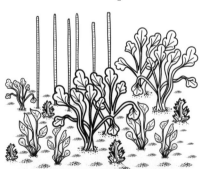

If you don't have access to a small patch of land, try creating a herb garden in a window box.

DATE you planted your vegetable patch:

_ _

WHAT veggies did you put into your patch?

_ _

As your vegetable patch **GROWS,** draw or stick in photos of the plants progressing.

Date: _ _ _ _ _ _ _ _ _ _ _ _   Date: _ _ _ _ _ _ _ _ _ _ _ _

Date: _ _ _ _ _ _ _ _ _ _ _ _   Date: _ _ _ _ _ _ _ _ _ _ _ _

VISITING A LANDMARK

It's time for a **trip!** Go with friends or family to visit a well-known landmark that you've never seen before.

Date:

Who did you go with?

Where did you go?

What landmark(s) did you see?

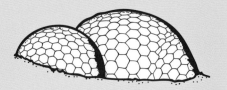

Draw a picture or stick in a
photo of the landmark here:

What was your **favourite thing** about going to visit
a landmark?

Where would you like to go **next**?

MAKING A MUSIC VIDEO

Are you ready to be a 9-year-old **video director** and **producer**? Have a go at planning and creating your very own music video.

What you will need

- Something to record the video with, like a phone or camera.
- Something to play music on, like a wireless speaker or laptop.
- An app or computer program for editing (optional).

SONG CHOICE

Which song will you make a music video for?

MUSIC VIDEO LOCATION

Where will you record your music video?

MUSIC VIDEO STARS

Who will be in the music video? It could be friends or family members, or you could **star** in the video too!

(You might need to make a stand for your camera or phone so that you can record yourself without holding it.)

MUSIC VIDEO 'CONCEPT'

What will **happen** in the music video? Will it tell a **story**? Will it show someone dancing or singing along to the song? Will it be serious and dramatic, sad, happy, or silly?

Now you have your music video plan, it is time to create it! It's a good idea to play the song **out loud** while you **film your video**, especially if people in the video will be singing or dancing in time to the music.

There are lots of phone apps and online computer programs that you could use to edit your music video once it is filmed – why not experiment to see what you could do? You could add the song over the top of the video, cut up different parts of it, make parts of the video go backwards, or play around with fun and colourful effects.

Once you are happy with your finished video, arrange a **viewing party** to show it to your family or friends!

Date:

What did you **enjoy most** about making a music video?

Are you **happy** with the finished video?

(What do you like and what could you improve?)

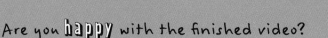

Who did you show the finished music video to?

Ask them to **rate** the video by colouring one of the emojis:

Now give the video **your rating**:

Would you like to make a music video again one day?

(If yes, what song would you choose next? If no, why not?)

RECIPE: **HOMEMADE PIZZA FACES**

Homemade pizza faces are so much **fun** because you can make them as **simple** or as **crazy** as you like! Why not invite a friend to try this recipe with you? You could even have a **pizza party**!

THE DOUGH

Ingredients

- 165g of strong white bread flour
- 165g of plain white flour, plus extra for kneading
- 3g of fast-action dried yeast
- 6g of salt
- 215ml of water
- 1 tablespoon of olive oil

How to make

1. Mix the flours together.
2. Add the salt and dried yeast to the flours. Combine.
3. Heat the water in a 800W microwave for 40 seconds.
4. Add the olive oil to the water.
5. Add the oil/water to the dry ingredients and mix well.
6. Tip the dough onto a lightly-floured work surface and knead the dough for about 12 minutes.
7. Coat the mixing bowl with a layer of plain flour.
8. Put the dough into the mixing bowl and seal with cling film.
9. Leave the dough to double in size (this can take 1–2 hours).
10. Tip the dough onto a floured work surface and divide into four, to make 4 medium-sized pizza bases.

BE SAFE!
Ask a grown-up to preheat the oven to 190°C/ Gas 5.

THE SAUCE

BE SAFE!
Ask a grown-up to help you when using tools like a knife, tin opener, pan or stove.

Ingredients

- 1 tin of chopped tomatoes
- 2 tablespoons of tomato puree or paste
- 1 crushed garlic clove
- 1 diced onion
- 1 tablespoon of olive oil
- 1 teaspoon of brown sugar
- 1 small handful of herbs like oregano or basil

How to make

1. Put the olive oil, onion and garlic into a pan and heat until soft.
2. Add the paste or puree, stir it and let it fry for a minute or two.
3. Put everything else into the pan and simmer for 15 mins.
4. Then turn the heat off and let the sauce cool down.
5. Once it has cooled, whizz it all up in a blender or food processor.
6. Now you can use a spoon to spread the sauce all over your pizza base.

THE FACES

The final (and most fun) step is to use whatever pizza toppings you like to make your pizza faces. Here are some tasty ideas:

- Slices of tomato
- Olives
- Slices of courgette
- Chunks of ham or chicken
- Long strips of pepper
- Pineapple
- Sliced mushrooms
- Mozzarella/cheese

How to make

1. Arrange your toppings on your pizza base.
2. Pop it in the preheated oven, and cook for around 8 minutes.
3. When it's as crispy as you like, take it out... and enjoy!

Turn the page...

Date:

Where did you make this recipe?

Who did you make it with?

Rate each part of making your pizza faces.

Making the dough:

Making the pizza sauce:

Making the faces:

Rate
this recipe
out of 10

1=Yuck!
10=Yum!

What did your pizza faces **look like?**

Draw, or stick in a photo.

How did they **taste?**

What was your **favourite** thing about making homemade pizza faces? Will you do it again?

MARBLING PAPER

Use colourful ink to cover your paper in mystical, SWIRLING pattern designs. You might be surprised at what you create!

What you will need

- A big shallow tray (an empty plastic storage box or lid can work well)
- Marbling inks (or make your own by mixing food colouring with vegetable oil)
- Paper (watercolour paper is best but any paper will work, just make sure you have a lot of it because you probably won't want to stop!)
- Something to cover your table such as newspaper or an old tablecloth
- Gloves (optional)
- Cocktail sticks (or a fork)
- A jug and some water

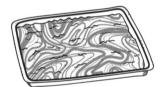

How to make

1. Cover your table with newspaper or an old tablecloth to stop it from getting too messy.
2. Put your tray on the table and half-fill the tray with water.
3. Add a few drops of ink into the water. Experiment with different colours. If you want pastel-coloured paper, only use small amounts of ink. If you'd like bright, colourful paper, use a bit more!
4. Use your cocktail sticks or a fork to swirl the water around, mixing the inks together and making them dance!
5. Lay a sheet of paper on top of the water.
6. Let it float for just a few seconds, then carefully peel it back and look at the incredible pattern you just created.
7. Put the paper somewhere to dry, then repeat as many times as you like...

Date: ....

WHERE did you marble paper? (And **WHO WITH**?)

....

What did you **ENJOY** about marbling paper?

....

Stick a bit of your marbled paper here.

Rate this activity:

SCHOOL TRIPS

Think of your favourite school trip so far — it could be an overnight stay or just a class day trip.

WHERE did you go?

Write or draw your answers.

What did you **DO**?

WHO did you spend the most time with?

What was your **FAVOURITE** part of the trip?

Do you have any photos from this school trip or other school trips you liked? Stick them here and **DECORATE** the frames.

Or you can draw!

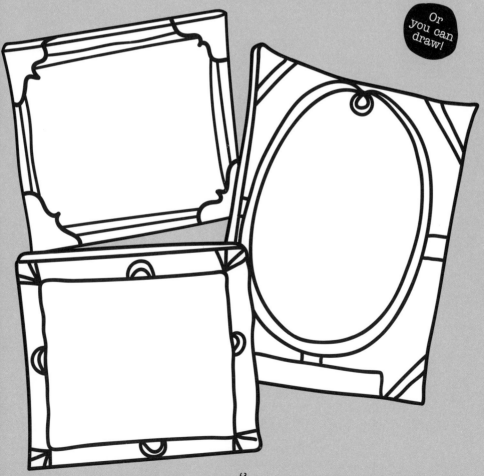

MY FAVOURITE FILM

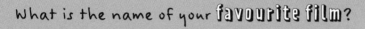

What is the name of your **favourite film**?

_____

What is the film about? Write a film **synopsis**
(a short description of what happens).

_____

_____

_____

_____

Why is it your **favourite** film?

_____

_____

If you could be any **character** in the film,
which one would you be?

_____

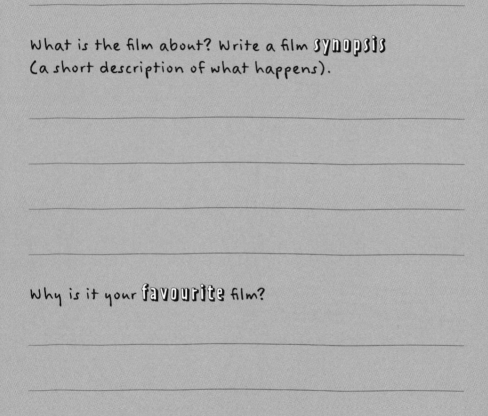

BEING A 9-YEAR-OLD FILM CRITIC

Whenever you watch a new film, write down the name of it and fill in your own **film review**.

Name of film	My rating (colour in the stars)	My review (what did you like or not like about it?)
	☆☆☆☆☆	
	☆☆☆☆☆	
	☆☆☆☆☆	
	☆☆☆☆☆	

SPORTS SUPERSTAR

What are your **TOP 3** favourite sports, exercises,
or fitness activities?

(If you don't have favourites, just pick a few that you like at the moment.)

① . . . .

② . . . .

③ . . . .

WHY do you like these sports or fitness activities so much?

_____

_____

If you could be a **PROFESSIONAL SPORTS** player when you
grow up, which **SPORT** would you like to play and why?

_____

_____

_____

MY TEAM

Write down the name of your favourite **SPORTS TEAM**.

(This could be any kind of team, whether it's a famous sports team that you support or a team that you play for as part of a sports club.)

WHAT KIND of sport does this team play?

WHY are they your favourite team?

Draw your favourite team's **LOGO**. If they don't have one, make one up!

Draw it or stick in a photo.

ON HOLIDAY

Think of a **holiday** or special **trip** you have been on in the past year.

Where did you go?

Write your answers, draw, or stick in photos.

Who did you go with?

What did you **take** with you?

What did you **do**?

What was your **favourite part** of the holiday or trip?

If you could plan your **dream** holiday or trip, **where** would you go and what would you do?

VISITING A WATERFALL

Some **waterfalls** are very high and truly impressive, some of them are surrounded by **pools** for swimming outdoors, and some of them can only be reached by walking long and winding **secret paths**.

Ask a grown-up to help you find a waterfall that you can travel to and visit, and record your **experience** here...

Date:

What waterfall did you visit? **Where** was it?

Who did you go with?

How did you **get there?**

What did the waterfall **look like?**

What was your **favourite** thing about visiting the waterfall?

MY TEACHERS

Your teachers always give you a report about how you are doing at school, so now it's your turn to **WRITE THEIR REPORT**!

REPORT CARD

(A+)

Name of your teacher:

. . . .

What do you **like best** about them?

. . . .

What are they really **good at**?

. . . .

What advice would you give your teacher about how they could **improve**?

. . . .

. . . .

Who has been your **favourite** teacher so far and why?

....

....

....

If you were the teacher of your class, what would you do?
Do you think it would be a **fun job** or a **difficult job**? Why?

....

....

....

....

....

MY 15 MINUTES OF FAME

If you could **switch lives** with someone famous for a whole day, who would you switch lives with?

Why did you choose that person?

Imagine you wake up tomorrow morning and you are that famous person for one day. Write a **short story** about what you think that day would be like.

Here are some ideas of what to write about.

What would you eat or drink?

How do you think people would treat you?

What would be the good and bad parts of being that famous person?

What would you do differently?

What would you still do the same?

MY PETS

Do you have any **pets**?

If **YES**, choose one and fill out the pet fact file below!

If **NO**, fill out the fact file below for the pet you would love to have!

Name: ....

Type of animal: ....

What does it **look like**?

Draw it or stick in a photo.

Do you think different pets have different **personalities**? Why or why not?

Draw your **dream pet** and where it would live...

(Would it live in an amazing tank? A giant hutch?)

How would you look after it?

NATURAL HISTORY EXPLORER

Dinosaurs, extinct animals, fossils, plants, and more — natural history is fascinating!

There are many museums with natural history sections. Ask a grown-up to help find one near you.

While you're there, see how many natural history explorer challenges you can complete.

Date: _____

What is the name of the museum you visited?

_____

Where is it?

_____

Who did you go with?

_____

_____

CHALLENGE 1: Big bones

Find a bone or fossil (bonus points if it is bigger than you!).

What is it? _____

Where is it from? _____

How old is it? _____

Draw it or stick in a photo.

CHALLENGE 2: Absolutely ancient

See if you can discover the oldest thing in the museum!
(You might have to explore for a while to find it, or maybe you could ask a museum guide for help.)

What is it? _____

Where is it from ? _____

How old is it? _____

Draw it or stick in a photo.

CHALLENGE 3: Faraway discoveries

Find something in a different language or that comes from a country you've never been to before.

What is it? _____

Where is it from? _____

How old is it? _____

Draw it or stick in a photo.

CHALLENGE 4: Subzero

Find what you think is the coolest thing in the museum.

What is it? _____

Where is it from ? _____

How old is it? _____

Draw it or stick in a photo.

CHALLENGE 5: Super souvenirs

Your last challenge is to cut and stick part of a museum souvenir into the box below.

(This could be something from a museum brochure, a sticker, part of a museum leaflet, your exhibition ticket or even a gift shop receipt.)

Or draw it if you prefer!

What was your favourite thing about your visit to the museum?

RECIPE: **APPLE PIE TURNOVERS**

Ingredients

- 3 medium apples
- 1 lemon
- 75g of caster sugar
- 4 sheets of puff pastry
- 30g of unsalted butter
- 1 egg (only the yolk)
- 1 tablespoon of milk
- 2 tablespoons of sultanas or raisins (optional)
- A pinch of cinnamon

BE SAFE!
Ask a grown-up for help with this recipe.

How to prepare

1. Preheat the oven to 200°C (Gas 6).
2. Use some butter to grease a baking tray or line it with baking paper, then pop it to one side.
3. Peel the apples, remove their cores, and chop them into small chunks.
4. Zest the lemon.

How to make

1. On a medium heat, melt the butter in a saucepan, then put the apples, lemon zest (plus the raisins and/or cinnamon if you're using them) into the pan.
2. Stir gently for 5 minutes until the apples are soft.
3. Take the pan off the heat and leave it to cool.
4. Meanwhile, lay the pastry out onto a tray and cut each sheet into 4 squares.
5. Put a big spoonful of your apple mixture into the middle of each square, then sprinkle with sugar.
6. Use a pastry brush to brush the edges of each square with a little bit of water.
7. Fold one corner of each square over to the other side, making a turnover shape.
8. Press the edges together with a fork to make a cool pattern!
9. Put your turnovers onto the baking tray you prepared earlier.
10. Mix the milk and egg yolk together and use the pastry brush to spread a thin layer over each turnover.
11. Sprinkle whatever sugar you have left over the top of the turnovers.
12. Bake them in the oven for 15–20 minutes, until they have puffed up and turned a delicious golden brown.
13. Remember to let them cool for at least 15 minutes before eating.

Date:

WHO did you make this recipe with?

Turn the page...

What did your apple turnovers **LOOK LIKE**?

Stick a photo here, or draw them!

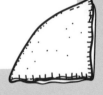

How did they **TASTE**?

What was your **FAVOURITE THING** about making this recipe?

Rate this recipe out of 10

1=Yuck!
10=Yum!

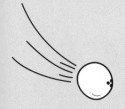

BOWLING

Did you know that there are at least 5 different types of bowling?

Whether it's 5-pin, 9-pin, 10-pin, candlepin, or duckpin bowling, take a trip to your nearest bowling alley and enjoy a game with friends or family!

Or set up your own bowling alley at home with bottles!

Date:

Where did you go bowling?

Who did you go with?

Which type of bowling did you do?

Who won?

Rate this experience out of 10

1=Awful
10=Awesome

MISSION: **HOW IT'S MADE**

YOUR MISSION: can you find out how something is made?

Maybe you could plan a factory tour trip with your family, or you could even ask your teacher if your class could go on an interesting school trip.

Here are some **ideas** for places to visit where you can find out how something is made:

- Art studio
- Car or transport factory
- Chocolate or sweets factory
- Clothes or toy manufacturers
- Film set
- Glassworks
- Pottery workshop
- TV studio

Date:

WHERE did you go?

WHO did you go with?

Fill in the **FINDINGS** from your mission on the next page.

HOW _____ **IS/ARE MADE**

Draw or write about the process of how it's made,
or stick in photos.

Continue on the blank pages at the end of this book if you like!

What was the **BEST** or **MOST INTERESTING** thing about
this mission?

GAMES NIGHT MARATHON

Plan an **EPIC** games night
with your family or friends!

All you'll need

- A cosy place for the evening
- Some tasty snacks and drinks as refreshments
- All your favourite games. These could be:
  - Board games of all different kinds
  - Card games like snap, Top Trumps® or UNO®
  - Family games like charades or Pictionary®
  - Video games on your computer or games console
    (multiplayer will work best!)

Date: _____

WHO did you have your games night marathon with?

_____

WHERE was it?

_____

What **REFRESHMENTS** did you have?

_____

LIST all the games you played and how long you played them for.

-

-

-

-

-

-

-

Which was your **FAVOURITE GAME** of the night? Why?

_____

_____

Rate your games night marathon:

MY FAMILY TREE

How much of your family tree can you fill in?

Add your name to the box that says 'Me!', then see how far back you can go.

(You might need to ask some of your family members for help.)

Date:

What was the most **difficult** thing about filling out your family tree and why?

What was the most **interesting** thing you found out while investigating your family tree?

Me!

SUPERCOOL SCIENCE EXPERIMENT

Water turns into a solid when it **FREEZES** below 0°C, right? Well actually, that's not always true!

Liquids need two things to become **solid ice** – **freezing cold** temperature and a 'nucleation site'.

A **nucleation site** is simply something that helps the ice crystals to form and grow.

When you put tap water or mineral water into the freezer it usually contains small **particles of minerals** that can act as **nucleation sites** to help the water form crystals and turn into ice.

TIP 1
You could also try opening your bottle of supercooled water and pouring it onto an ice cube – it will turn into instant ice!

For this easy but impressive science experiment, put a few bottles of purified water (water that is filtered to take out things like minerals) into your freezer for around 2 hours. (Don't open the freezer in that time, it needs to cool slowly!)

With freezing temperatures but no nucleation sites, you will be able to create supercooled water.

This means that you can take the water out of the freezer and even though it is freezing it will still be a liquid... until you hit it! Hit the bottom of the water bottle on a table and watch it turn to solid ice instantly.

TIP 2
If your water doesn't supercool, try leaving it for a bit longer. If it freezes too quickly, let it melt then try again for a shorter time.

Date: _____

Did you **SUPERCOOL** the water on your first try?
(Or did you have to make some changes to your experiment first?)

_____

How did you **FEEL** when you watched the supercooled
water turn to instant ice?

_____

What was your **FAVOURITE** thing about this experiment?

_____

Why not **FILM** a video of your supercool science
experiment and show it to a friend or family member?
WRITE down what they thought here:

_____

_____

_____

_____

 _____

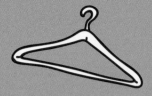

MY STYLE

Describe your fashion 'style' in 3 words:

1 _____

2 _____

3 _____

What outfit are you wearing today?

What is your favourite outfit to wear?

Draw, write, or stick in a photo.

BEING A 9-YEAR-OLD
FASHION DESIGNER

DESIGN an outfit for your **FAVOURITE CELEBRITY** to wear.

(This could be an outfit for your favourite singer to wear in a **music video**, an outfit for your favourite actor to wear on the **red carpet**, or even a sports kit for your **favourite player** to wear!)

You can draw, or even stick bits of material to the page if you'd like.

MY PHOTOGRAPHY CHALLENGE

You can draw instead of sticking in photos if you prefer.

Get a **CAMERA** ready, because it's time for your photography challenge! When you have completed each task, stick in the photo.

Task 1

Take a photo of the same **TREE** in 2 different seasons.

Task 2

Take a photo of a **WILD ANIMAL** in its natural habitat.

Task 3

Take a photo of a **CLOUD** that looks like something else.

(Label what it looks like.)

Task 4

Take a photo of something **REFLECTED** in water.

Task 5

WALK 50 STEPS from where you are right now and take a photo of what you find there.

Task 6

Take portrait photos of 4 people who are **IMPORTANT** to you.

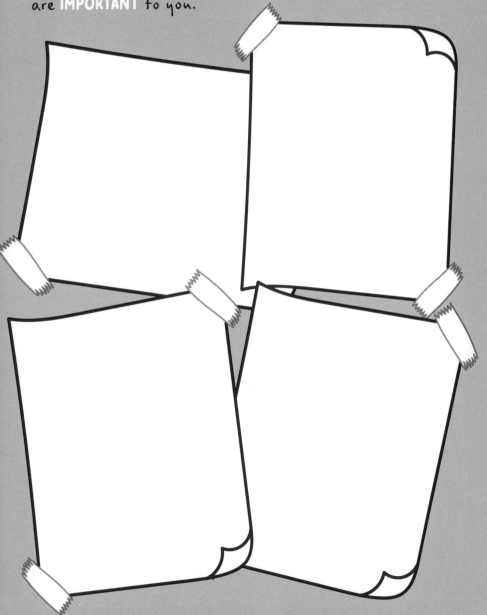

MY THEATRE EXPERIENCE

You might be surprised how much is going on in theatres. You can often see plays, pantomimes, ballets, music concerts, comedy and circus shows.

Ask a family member to help you plan a **VISIT** to the theatre **OR** simply make your very **OWN** theatre at home and put on a performance!

Date: ....

If you visited a theatre, write its **NAME** here. If you made your own theatre, make up a name for it!

....

What did you **SEE** or **PERFORM** at the theatre?

....

....

Rate the experience:

Use this space to **DRAW** the theatre or performance, or even stick in a ticket!

What was the **BEST THING** about your theatre experience?

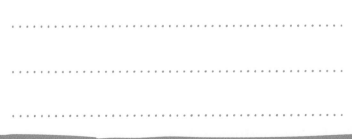

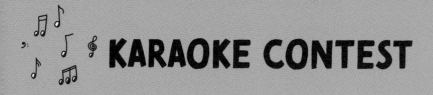

KARAOKE CONTEST

It doesn't matter whether you're an **amazing** singer or a **rubbish** singer, you can still have a **karaoke contest**!

- All you need is something to play music on, and some other people who are willing to take part.

- Each person should choose 2 or 3 songs they would like to sing along to, then you can take it in turns to perform 1 song each.

- You can sing along to the normal version of the song, or you could search online for the 'karaoke version' of each song (which will have no singing in it and usually has the words on the screen for you to follow).

Turn it into a proper contest with prizes for the best singer, best performance, and funniest song!

Date:

Where did you have your karaoke contest?

Who **joined in?**

What songs did you sing?

What was the **best** (or funniest) thing about the karaoke contest?

Who won the karaoke contest?

Rate this activity:

HOST YOUR OWN SPORTS DAY

Sports days at school are fun, but it's even more fun to host one of your own. Here's what you need to plan...

LOCATION

You could host your sports day in a garden, local park or field. Just make sure you ask permission to use the space.

Where will your sports day be?

_____

ATHLETES

You could host a family sports day, you could invite your friends to take part, or maybe you could have a mix of family and friends.

Who will you invite to take part in your sports day?

_____

_____

_____

_____

DATE

Check what date will be best for you and the other athletes.
Summer is usually a good time to choose.

When will you host your sports day?

SPORTS

There are loads of different games, sports, or races you could do.
What would you and the other people taking part enjoy most?

What sports will you include?

Here are some **ideas**:

- Running race
- Hopping race
- Obstacle course
- Egg-and-spoon race
- Sack race
- Wheelbarrow race
- Three-legged race
- Hula hoop challenges
- Space hopper race
- Mini tennis tournament
- Hurdles
- Volleyball
- Relay race
- Balloon games
- Bean-bag-throwing competition
- Five-a-side football
- Dribbling a football around cones
- A mini triathlon of different skills

PRIZES

Though it is true that it's the taking part that counts, everyone loves competing for the chance to win an amazing prize. Why not get some fun prizes for the winners and runners-up of each event, or maybe you could give medals and certificates?

What prizes will you give?

REFRESHMENTS

With all of this activity going on, you'll want to make sure that everyone taking part can refuel! Ask a grown-up if they can help you prepare some drinks and healthy snacks ready for the day.

What refreshments will you make?

ON THE DAY

What were the best things about hosting your own sports day? What went well?

What would you improve if you hosted another sports day?

Draw or stick in a photo of something great that happened at your sports day.

MY FAVOURITE GAME

What is your favourite **GAME**?

What is the game about? **HOW** do you play it?

WHO do you normally play it with?

WHY is it your favourite game?

How does playing this game make you **FEEL**?

GAME TRACKER

Every time you play a **GAME** that you like, write down the name of it here, along with the reason why you like it.

Date	Game	Why I like it

WATCHING THE SUNSET

Sunsets are **awesome** and they happen every single day! But, even though it's easy to do, not many of us really take a minute to stop and **watch** a sunset.

Plan out your own sunset viewing here:

Date:

What is the weather like **today**?
(Remember, a clear day is best for watching a sunset.)

Where will you **watch** the sunset from?
(Usually somewhere quite high up, like a hill or a top-floor window is a good place to see the sunset, just make sure that it faces west!)

What **time** will the sun set today?
(The time of the sunset will be different depending on where you live and what time of year it is. Find out when the sun will set in your area.)

Who will you watch the sunset with?

Draw what the sunset looks like in its **different stages**, or stick in some photos.

WHEN I GROW UP...

Thinking about growing up is weird.
People always ask you what you'd like
to do as a job... but what about everything else?!

If you do have an idea of what future career you'd like,
write it below. If not, don't worry — that's OK!

Instead of talking about what you want to be, let's talk
about who you want to be. What kind of person would
you like to be when you grow up?

When I grow up, I'd like to be a person who:

...helps
other people?
...leads other
people?
Something
else?

Who inspires you? Are there any adults you admire that you would like to be similar to when you grow up?

Draw them here, or write down why you would like to be like them.

MAKING A VISION BOARD

Have you ever made a **vision board** or a **moodboard**? They are giant collage boards that aren't just fun to make, they also help you **set and reach your goals**!

What you will need

- A large cork board and some pins
   OR a large piece of card and some glue
- Magazines or newspapers you can cut things out of
- A laptop or computer and printer (optional)
- Pens, coloured paper, tape, stickers, and any other decorations

How to make

Maybe something from pages 11 or 114-115?

1. First, decide what you would like to include on your vision board. What are your goals? Is there anything you'd like to achieve?
2. Now you've decided what you'd like to include, look through the magazines and newspapers to find pictures and words that could represent your goals. You could also search for pictures online and print them out.
3. Now it is time to arrange your vision board. Cut out your pictures and words, then pin them onto the cork board or use glue to stick them to your large piece of card.
4. Once it is complete, hang the vision board somewhere that you can look at it often. This isn't just so you can admire your masterpiece all the time, it's also so you can remind yourself of your goals and notice when you are working towards them!

Date:

What **goals** did you include on your vision board?

What did your finished board **look like**?

Stick a photo here, or draw it!

Where did you put up your vision board?

What was your **favourite thing** about making it?

MY AWESOME YEAR BEING 9

You can write, draw, or stick things in!

A NOTE TO GROWN-UPS

You can join in the fun too by sharing experiences together, discussing the activities and celebrating accomplishments throughout the year! And remember to help with some of the recipes and other tricky tasks.

Follow us on Instagram @Collins4Parents where we'll be hosting regular competitions and giveaways as well as giving you extra ideas to make the year **even more awesome!** Share your experiences with the book using the hashtag #MyAwesomeYearBeing

MY AWESOME YEAR SERIES

9780008372606   9780008372613

9780008372620   9780008372637   9780008372644

MY YEAR IN COLOUR

Each day this year, use this COLOUR TRACKER to record YOUR MOOD. Choose a colour for each mood and colour in the chart for each day. You could use more than one colour for a day if you like.

My mood is 😁 , today was AWESOME!

My mood is 😎 , today was cool.

My mood is 😍 , today was exciting!

My mood is 😆 , today was funny.

My mood is 😴 , today was tiring.

My mood is 😖 , today was confusing.

My mood is 🙁 , today was sad.

My mood is 😠 , today was annoying.

My mood is 😮 , today was scary.

⭐ Today is my BIRTHDAY!